HOW IT WAS

VICTORIAN TOWN LIFE

Michael Rawcliffe

B. T. Batsford Ltd, London

CONTENTS

© Michael Rawcliffe 1993

First published 1993

Typeset by Goodfellow & Egan, Ltd, Cambridge
and printed in Hong Kong
for the publishers
B. T. Batsford Ltd
4 Fitzhardinge Street
London W1H 0AH

ISBN 0 7134 6355 4

A CIP catalogue record for this book is available from the British Library.

The frontispiece shows a street juggler, of around 1865.

Street entertainment was very popular in Victorian times.

INTRODUCTION

Queen Victoria's reign covered a long period (1837–1901); more than many people's lives. Looking back from the standpoint of 1901 one would have seen many changes during this time. In 1837 railways were in their infancy, and the first railway linking two major cities had only opened seven years before, between Liverpool and Manchester. By 1901 the railway network covered the whole country, linking every town and city.

In 1837 the majority of people lived and worked in the countryside. London was by far the largest city, and only seven other towns had populations of over 100,000. By 1901 there were 40 towns as large. This process is called urbanization, and this book will look at its impact upon the people who lived at this time.

From 1851 the majority of people were classified as urban dwellers, but as the definition of a town was that it had 2,000 or more people, many were no more than overgrown villages, and many people still lived close to the countryside. In the second half of the century, industry began to spread more widely, and many of the northern towns, whose industry was based upon textiles, began rapidly to expand. However, it would be misleading to suggest that every town was industrial, and that every town dweller worked in a factory. Reading this book you will see the variety of different types of towns such as market, seaside, cathedral, mining, educational and ones which grew as ports. Many newcomers came to the towns seeking higher wages and regular work. Some went into the new factories, but many continued doing what they knew best: working in domestic service, in shops or in breweries; working with horses, or as carpenters, tailors, ordinary labourers or gardeners.

The rapidly increasing population of many of the towns led to problems of health, particularly for those who had to live near where they sought, or had, work. Here they were crowded into cheap and inadequate housing, and many towns simply could not cope. In time, those who could afford to took advantage of improved transport and moved into the growing suburbs. In many of the new towns the rich and the poor came to live apart.

It is hoped that this book will enable and encourage you to find out how your area developed during this period. Few Victorians still survive, but the Victorian period is particularly rich in sources of various kinds.

Many Victorian buildings and streets still exist, in spite of redevelopment, and the wealth of photographs, advertisements, directories and various other sources will tell you much about the people, as well as the way the towns and cities developed during this time.

OLD MONEY
There were: 240 pence (d) to a pound a sixpence (6d.) is 2½p a shilling (1s. or 1/-) is 5p half a crown (2s. 6d. or 2/6d.) is 12½p ten shillings (10s. or 10/-) is 50p

Introductory quiz

Do you know?

Which of the following towns was only a village in 1830? Liverpool, Middlesbrough, Leeds, Manchester?

Which disease was given the royal title of King?

What was a wake's week?

Which city had many wynds?

What do Mayhew, Booth and Rowntree have in common?

What is a back-to-back?

Why was the Manchester Ship Canal built?

What was a costermonger?

Where were villas usually built?

Which entertainment cost a penny?

Which disease killed 62,000 people in 1848–9?

What was the name of the pipe in the street which provided water?

VARIOUS TOWNS

London was, and is, Britain's largest city and its population more than doubled between 1837 and 1901. Migrants were attracted to it from all parts of the country. With improved transport, those who could moved out into less densely-populated areas or into the surrounding villages, travelling to and from London each day.

Interestingly, London's expansion was not based upon large factories, but rather on skills and crafts, and the industry was marked by smaller factories, workshops and work at home. Also it was a great port, the seat of government and a great financial and commercial centre, the natural terminus of all the major railway companies.

Manchester, one of the largest cities by the end of the century, was seen as the place of the future; a city which developed the factory system and where King Cotton ruled. The cotton industry was its main source of wealth and factories were built at a rapid rate as the century proceeded. To combat the high cost of importing raw cotton from Liverpool, the Manchester Ship Canal was built and opened in 1894. Manchester now became Britain's fourth largest port, as well as being a great commerical, financial and engineering centre.

Other Northern towns developed in East Lancashire, centred on the mill. The machinery was increasingly powered by steam, produced by coal

from the nearby pits. Oldham, Burnley, Rochdale and Colne all grew rapidly, and in the West Riding of Yorkshire the woollen industry also grew quickly, leading to the expansion of towns such as Bradford, Halifax and Leeds.

Towns developed for a variety of reasons. Sheffield had no railway before 1870, but nevertheless had a well-established iron and steel industry based upon a multitude of small workshops. The workers had highly developed skills, and water from the fast-flowing streams powered the wheels which turned the machinery. Equally, Birmingham continued to grow into the leading city of the Midlands. Its importance was not based upon the factory, but like Sheffield, upon the small workshops, which specialized in various metal products from toys to guns.

Other towns, such as Ipswich, Lincoln and Norwich developed as centres of agricultural regions. Each had well-established markets and two had cathedrals. They were to develop the skills which they knew best, such as brewing, producing agricultural machinery and corn milling, and as the century proceeded served not only their own region, but came to sell to other areas as well.

Other towns developed around the railway where individual companies had their repair yards and where engines and rolling stock were built, both for Britain and for export. In Kent, the market town of Ashford, which is now being transformed by the Channel Tunnel, was developed as the centre for the South Eastern Railway Company, and Alfred New Town was built on the outskirts to house the railway workers. Many of these came from the industrial North-East where there were already many experienced railway engineers. Similarly Swindon in Wiltshire became the centre for the Great Western Railway (GWR). By contrast, Crewe emerged from virtually nothing as the railway centre for the London Midland and Scottish Railway Company (LMS) and its name derived from that of the local landowner, the Earl of Crewe.

Shorter working hours, bank holidays and cheap railway travel led to the development of the seaside town. Many came to serve particular towns and regions – Blackpool and Morecambe in the north-west; Scarborough in Yorkshire; Skegness and Great Yarmouth in Lincolnshire and East Anglia; Eastbourne, Brighton, Margate and Ramsgate in the South-East. Each came to serve a particular group and class of visitor.

So by 1901 the vast majority of people lived either in towns or sufficiently near to be influenced by them. By 1901 four out of five people lived in urban areas and many features of our present urban life had emerged.

This picture of a London street scene was painted in 1884. How is it different from a similar scene today?

A Scotsman in Manchester

Hugh Miller was a Scotsman who made his first journey to England in 1845. Here he describes his first impressions of Manchester, before the one o'clock lunch bell:

> One receives one's first intimation [hint] of its existence from the lurid gloom of the atmosphere that overhangs it . . . And now the innumerable chimneys came in view, tall and dim in the dun [dull grey] haze, each bearing atop its own troubled pennan [point] of darkness. And now we . . . pass through mediocre streets of brick, that seem as if they were built wholesale by contract within the last half-dozen years. These humble houses are the homes of the operative [factory] workers. . . . We see whole streets of warehouses – dead, dingy, gigantic buildings – barred out from the light; and save where here and there a huge waggon stands, lading or unlading under the mid-air cranes, the thoroughfares . . . have a solitary half-deserted air.

(H. Miller *First Impressions of England and its People*, Edinburgh, 1857)

Q

Do you think that the writer is attracted by what he saw? What tells us that many of the houses were newly built?

CAN YOU REMEMBER ?

Why London was so important?
What was the name of the great Midland city?
What factory machinery was powered by?
Where the woollen industry was located?
Which railway company made Ashford important?

Birmingham in the 1890s. Note the Victorian developments in the centre, the railway station and the chimneys and smoke on the horizon.

CHECK YOUR UNDERSTANDING

Can you remember the meaning of the following words?

census
GWR
LMS
urban
rural

Rising Populations

	1831	1901
Bath	51,000	50,000
Norwich	61,000	112,000
York	26,000	78,000
Chester	21,000	38,000
Brighton	41,000	123,000
Blackpool	943	47,000
London	1.75m	4.5m
Manchester	182,000	544,000
Liverpool	202,000	685,000
Middlesbrough	154	91,000
Cardiff	6,000	164,000

(Source: *Census tables*)

With the help of an atlas divide these towns into various groups, e.g. industrial, port, seaside or market towns. As you read through this book you may be able to suggest reasons for the dramatic rise of some of the towns listed.

Try to find the population of your town during this period.

THINGS TO DO

It may be possible to build up a data-base of town populations and add census figures for the intervening years (e.g. 1871). If a fact file is available you could build up a profile of a large town, preferably your own. Include details such as population, occupations, date of the coming of the railway, major Victorian buildings, etc.

Even though the typical Briton in 1837 was neither a town dweller nor an industrial worker, the cotton industry was the largest and fastest growing of our industries. There were 200,000 workers in cotton mills (factories) in 1830, although they were outnumbered by ¼ million non-factory workers in the cotton industry alone. Of those in the cotton mills, half of the workers were women, and there were many children too.

In fact, the growth of factories boosted the traditional industries and crafts, and there were far more men working at home in sheds or on hand-looms than working in factories. However, the trend was against them. The hand-loom weaver working at home found himself unable to compete with the factory power-loom, increasingly operated by steam power.

By 1851 several cotton towns had emerged in East Lancashire centred on a large mill or mills. Many of these were still dependent on water-powered mills, but the use of steam was becoming increasingly common. Between 1801 and 1841 the population of Lancashire towns such as Blackburn, Burnley, Chorley and Preston increased by at least three times.

To the east of the Pennines in Yorkshire the woollen industry was also rapidly developed. Unlike cotton, it was a long established industry, and different areas of the county specialized in producing different types of cloth. The adoption of the factory system came later than in the cotton industry, and many towns such as Bradford and Leeds expanded as a result.

The working conditions and the long hours, especially for women, became a growing concern. In 1833 a Factory Act was passed which restricted the age and hours which children and women could work. The Act was to be supervised by only four inspectors, but in time their numbers were increased. Further factory acts followed but by 1850 between 60 and 70 hours a week was still the average for adults, and it was not for another 20 years that cotton workers and engineers achieved a 54 to 56½-hour week. The rest of industry gained it by the 1880s. In time factory-based industry came to be subject to laws regarding conditions and safety at work, enforced by inspectors.

The Great Exhibition of 1851 demonstrated the lead Britain had over all its competitors. On display were the products of the world's industry, with Britain regarded as 'the workshop of the world'.

In 1888 Wymans produced a commercial encyclopaedia in which the country's leading firms were described. Typical entries included:

Huntley and Palmers Biscuit Manufacturers, Reading	3,000–4,000 workers
Howlett and White, Boot and Shoe Manufacturers, Norwich	1,000 workers ¾ million shoes made a year
Bass, Ratcliff and Gretton, Brewers, Burton-on-Trent	2,250 workers
Price's Patent Candle Company, London	1,500 workers
Macfarlane, Strong and Company, Cast Iron Pipe Manufacturers, Glasgow	'at present completing an order for 25,000 tons of pipes for Manchester Corporation'
Joseph Rodgers and Sons, Cutlers, Sheffield	2,000 workers
R.E. Crompton, Electricians, Chelmsford	600 workers
North British Rubber Company, Edinburgh – tyre producers	900–1,000 workers
Neilson Locomotive Engineers, Glasgow	1,000 workers

As this list shows many of the tasks which had been done at home or in the small workshop were now done more cheaply in factories with large machinery. The production of machinery and machine tools and parts were also industries in themselves.

Many firms came to have head offices in London and the major cities, and the number of new firms and factories expanded to cope with the increasing demand, not ony for traditional goods, but also for new ones such as gas fittings, sewing-machines, typewriters and electric light bulbs. In addition, many firms became large exporters through the growing ports, and others processed tropical fruits and foods which were now cheaper and more readily available through the canning and milling industries.

Inside a Birmingham Ironworks. Tapping the pig iron from the furnace was both skilled and dangerous. Note how the men wear no protective clothing.

Factory Children

Various enquiries into children's working conditions were set up by Parliament. In 1832 Samuel Coulson, father of two girls who worked in a Leeds mill, was interviewed by the select committee:

Q **At what time in the morning, in the brisk [busy] time, did those girls go to the mills?**

A **In the brisk time, for about six weeks, they have gone at 3 o'clock in the morning, and ended at 10, or nearly half-past at night.**

Q **What intervals were allowed for rest or refreshment during those 19 hours of labour?**

A **Breakfast a quarter of an hour, and dinner half an hour, and drinking a quarter of an hour.**

Q **What was the length of time they could be in bed during those long hours?**

A **It was near 11 o'clock before we could get them into bed after getting a little victuals [food] and then my mistress used to stop up all night for fear we could not get them ready in time.**

One of the parents got up at 2 a.m. to dress the children. The busy time lasted about 6 weeks a year. The rest of the year the hours were from 6 a.m. 'til 8.30 p.m. They were paid 3/- a day and 7½d more when it was busy.

Q **Had any of them any accident in consequence of this labour?**

A **Yes, my eldest daughter when she first went there . . . the cog caught her forefinger nail and screwed it off below the knuckle, and she was five weeks in Leeds Infirmary [hospital].**

(Report of Select Committee on Factory Children's Labour, 1831–32)

As soon as the accident happened the wages were totally stopped and the children were both strapped (beaten) for being tired. They were not allowed to sit down whilst at work.

The children were paid only for the hours they worked. If they worked six days a week how many hours would they work in the 'brisk' time, and how many during the remaining weeks? Roughly how much were they paid each hour? Why do you think that young children were so useful in the mill?

CAN YOU REMEMBER ?

What was the fastest growing industry in 1837?
Why was the Factory Act of 1833 so important?
Why was the Great Exhibition held?
Which city produced the highest-quality steel goods?

Women at work in a Lancashire cotton mill c. 1910.

Thomas Wood, Engineer

Thomas was born in Bingley, Yorkshire and was the son of a hand-loom weaver. After serving an apprenticeship as an engineer, he moved to Platt Brothers in Oldham, one of the largest textile machinery makers. He worked on the latest Whitworth machine tools and gauges, earning 32/- a week.

> It was with a fear of an indefinite something that I commenced work for a firm who employed near 2,000 hands [workers], whose tools were mostly Whitworth's make – I, who had never worked in a [work] shop with more than eight or ten men and with country-made tools, the very best of which Platts would have thrown away as utterly useless . . .
>
> . . . I saw many start that they paid off [sacked] the first day, some at an even shorter trial. I determined to do my best . . .
>
> (*The Autobiography of Thomas Wood* 1822–1880. Quoted in J. Burnett (ed) *Useful Toil* Allen Lane, 1974)

What would be the great advantage of Whitworth tools? Why was Thomas so worried on his first day?

The Potter

The Potters of the Midlands suffered from many diseases. The fine dust from the bones, flints and clays damaged their lungs, the constant high temperatures led to rheumatism and the use of lead poisoned them. A doctor at the North Staffordshire Infirmary in Stoke-on-Trent in 1860 reported that:

> The potters, as a class, both men and women, represent a degenerated [rundown] population . . . They are as a rule stunted in growth, ill-shaped and ill-formed in the chest. They are certainly short-lived; . . . of all the diseases they are especially prone to chest diseases, to pneumonia, bronchitis, and asthma. One form would appear peculiar to them, that which is known as potters' asthma or potters' consumption.
>
> *(Parliamentary Papers 1861)*

Generations of families had worked in this highly-skilled industry. Even when the risks to their health were understood many workers refused to use safety equipment such as masks. Why do you think this was?

CHECK YOUR UNDERSTANDING

Can you remember the meaning of the following words?

brewer
canning and milling
cast iron
cutler
machine tools

The river Don in Sheffield c. 1884. Why do you think industry was often situated alongside rivers?

THINGS TO DO

1 The Select Committee evidence is best read aloud. Use the extract in this section, and other similar material.

2 Check the directories for your town, or the nearest area, to see whether industry was important then. With the aid of a large-scale Ordnance Survey (OS) map try to locate the industries. Go and see whether the buildings still survive, and whether they house the same industries. In the North many textile mills have now been closed.

WORKING IN THE HOME

Many women had traditionally worked at home, and continued to do so after the growth of the factory system and the rapid expansion of towns and cities. Even at the end of the nineteenth century every town had a substantial number of people who worked at home or in workshops, rather than in large groupings in factories, mines or offices.

However, their position was changing, and frequently for the worse. The group whose standard of living fell dramatically with the introduction of the power-loom in the factory, was that of the hand-loom weaver. By the 1840s they were on a starvation wage of about one penny an hour, unable to compete with the cheaper, factory-woven cloths. Compare this with the 30/- 35/- a week

The Song of the Shirt by Frank Holl. Needlewomen who worked at home were often worse off than those in workshops. Hours were long with low pay and no security of employment.

which was earned by skilled workers in 1800. Nevertheless, in the 1851 census, workers such as these were still the third largest group after agricultural labourers and domestic servants.

Today, many women have paid work in addition to unpaid housework. This was even more the case in the nineteenth century. Women and children formed the bulk of the work-force in the textile industry, but the largest occupation for women was domestic service. A large number of unmarried girls between 13 and 18 years old went to work 'in service' for others, 'living in', away from home. In the villages surrounding the growing Kent suburb of Bromley many girls left home to work for others. Tradesmen in the town might employ a girl who did most of the household tasks, either assisting the wife or housekeeper. They were usually described as 'maids of all work' or 'servant girls' on the census return. Higher up the scale, the middle class, in their new suburban villas, might employ two or three servants. In the large detached house, the rich employed six or more servants, including a butler, coachman, groom, housekeeper, lady's servant, chambermaid, scullery maid and perhaps a nurse or governess. By the 1870s a servants' recruitment agency had been established in the Market Square. In addition, the specialist servants were advertised nationally in papers such as *The Times*, whilst the young servant girl might follow her elder sister into service, or her parents might respond to a local advertisement. Pay varied according to position, but as servants lived in and had their food provided, it was very little. Hours were very long, and days off were few. Servants usually lived in the attics and ate and prepared the meals in the kitchens 'below stairs' in the basement.

Widows or older women would often work at home as washerwomen or as child minders. They were usually from the poorer groups who needed every penny that could be earned.

In the 1830s a new word was coined – 'sweating'. It was used to describe the individual, working either at home, or in a small workshop, who worked for very low wages, and for very long hours, doing such thing as shirt-making, button-stitching, dressmaking, matchbox-making or brush-making.

In Nottingham and Leicester the framework stocking knitters and the lace-makers continued outside the factory system until the 1860s and 1870s, but they were fighting a losing battle. What made conditions in these trades worse was that they were not covered by the Factory Acts until 1867 when legislation was extended to small factories and workshops. Work at home in the sweated industries was not covered until 1909.

Home workers were usually paid by the number of items completed, or 'piece'. Piece rates were determined by the buyer or the small employer in the workshop and the individual had no rights or bargaining powers. Often the home worker had to buy basics such as pins, scissors, glue, etc. and sometimes actual materials. If a machine was used, such as a framework knitting machine, it was usually rented and that also reduced the amount one could earn. With the invention of the sewing-machine in the second half of the century sweating in the garment industry increased.

From the 1850s, many journalists and investigators reported on the plight of the poorly-paid workers. Charles Dickens in his magazine *Household Words* and Henry Mayhew in his articles in the *Morning Chronicle* graphically described their conditions. In the 1880s a major survey was begun by Charles Booth who gave many details of the conditions of the poor in the East End of London. It included much on the workers in the sweated industries.

In 1888 Beatrice Webb went to work in a sweat shop in order to report on the conditions. She published her findings on conditions in the garment industry in the journal *The Nineteenth Century* and she also gave evidence before a House of Lords Select Committee on the Sweating Industry in the East End. In speaking of the tailoring trade in London she said that the hours of work were from '8 or 7 half past in the morning till 10 or 11 at night'.

What particularly shocked was not only that many of these unfortunate workers were working long hours in dangerous conditions for very little money, they were also sweating in order to provide expensive clothing for the whole range of society, including the very rich.

Children at Work

The following is taken from an article *'One Dinner a Week'* written by a reporter in the East End of London in 1884 who talked to those queueing for soup in a church hall.

> (He) told me, with some pride, that he could weekly add some six or seven shillings to the family support by working every day about ten hours at a stretch. To fix the bristles in a scrub-brush is a slow way to grow rich, for you only gain a penny if you fill two hundred holes, and you will soon find that your fingers suffer from the work. Nor is making match-boxes a lucrative employment when you are paid two-pence a gross (144) for them, providing your own paste.
>
> (*All the Year Round*, 16 February 1884)

The Machinist

Another article entitled *'Travels in the East'* appeared the next month in the same magazine.

> Her machine was on the table, . . . piled upon a chair, and put quite ready to her hand, lay a lot of little pieces of thickish grey tweed cloth, shaped as the two sides of what in the cheap clothing lists are recorded as 'boys' vests'. These were to be sewn, and neatly fitted to the back.
>
> . . . She had to put the buttons on, and to press the work, when finished. And she also had to pay for the hire of the machine, and to buy her needles too, she had, and pay for her own thread. Sewing pretty steadily from seven in the morning until nine or so at night, merely stopping for her meals, and not long for them either, she could manage pretty well to make three waistcoats in a day, and she was paid sometimes sixpence, sometimes sevenpence a piece.

What is the man on the right collecting? How does his manner contrast with that of the family? (Punch 1883)

Homeworkers in West Ham

In 1905 a detailed survey was carried out into the problems of a poor London Borough. The poorer areas contained many home workers. Amongst the poorest were the sack workers and brush workers.

(They) are usually women of a very poor class, and in a considerable number of cases their husbands are, or have lately been, irregular workers ... sack makers often complain that the work is very hard, and that their hands are cut by the tar rope and by the coarse needles.

Brush working is apt to be dangerous when carried on as home work. As the kitchen is often used as a work-room, the bristles may come into contact with food, and all the members of the family are exposed to the dangers of anthrax.

Sack makers earned 1s. 8d. per 100 sacks.

Hairbrush makers from 1s. 8d. to 2s. 11d. according to the number of holes.

(*West Ham,* ed. E.G. Howarth and M. Wilson Dent, 1907)

Slave Labour in Birmingham

Conditions were little better at the end of Victoria's reign. Robert Sherard described home work by the Birmingham poor:

Back of Richard Street I found a woman and a little girl; ... who were dying of starvation in the hook-and-eye trade. 'Starting', she said, 'the two of us early on Saturday morning and working hard all day Saturday, and beginning again on Monday morning and on till dinner-time, we earned 1/6d. You get 10d. for a pack, and you find your own cotton and needles. Me and my little girl (the only one of five old enough to work) – worked yesterday from 4.30 p.m. till past 11, and we earned 4d. between us. None of these people had eaten anything all that day. There was only a little tea and sugar in the house. The babies were crying.
(R Sharard *'The Child-Slaves of Britain'*, first published by *The London Magazine* in 1905)

Why do you think so many people worked in the 'sweated industries'?

In any large town or city in Victorian times the streets would have been full of people. These would have included those selling specialist goods such as flowers, roast chestnuts, birds, fruit and vegetables, as well as cab drivers and policemen. The goods would usually have been prepared at home, and there are many descriptions of the homes of the poor where in the single rented room, or cellar dwelling, vegetables would be prepared for selling. Later the unsold items would be stacked in the same room at the end of the day. The sellers of fruit and vegetables were known as costermongers, and they would usually own or rent a handcart from which they would sell their produce. Each specialist would have his cry: 'Flowers, penny a bunch!', 'Knives to grind!', 'Hot spice gingerbread!' 'O(ld) Clo(thes)!'. 'New laid eggs, eight a groat (4d.) – crack 'em and try 'em!'

In many towns and cities there were street markets and the poor would often shop late on a Saturday night when food, especially meat, would be sold off cheaply. Certain streets had reputations for selling particular things such as clothes, fruit, vegetables or live birds or animals. These are often remembered in names such as Milk Street, Petticoat Lane or Pudding Lane, where the goods were either made or sold.

Many towns had risen to importance by being granted the right to hold markets. Markets were still important and cities such as London had specialist ones to which goods and animals would be brought in from the countryside. Drovers brought cattle and sheep along the drove or green roads into London's Smithfield Market. One of the improvements carried out by the Victorians, after the railways enabled a greater variety of food to be brought by rail from a greater distance, was the building of new covered markets. Hence Billingsgate, Smithfield and Covent Garden were rebuilt. In Leeds and Halifax the impressive Victorian markets and shopping arcades still do a thriving trade.

In spite of the railway and the opportunity to bring in fresh milk daily by train, old rural habits still persisted. In 1847 it was reported that there were 14 cow-sheds in Westminster, and that in one alone, 40 cows were kept. The conclusion was that much of the milk sold on the London streets was a danger to health, but it was still being sold on the London streets in the 1860s.

One might have expected that the railway would have led to the end of horse-drawn traffic. However, this was far from the case, and by 1900 there were more horses being used than in 1800. They were used to take people between stations, and throughout the urban areas. Some of these were on established omnibus routes, pulling various

types of carriages. Goods were also transported throughout towns and cities: large shire-horses would pull huge carts containing barrels of beer while second-hand clothes sellers would take their old mares or donkeys around the streets. The horse was a major occupation. Grooming, feeding and riding as well as crossing sweepers were all important until the advent of the petrol engine in the early twentieth century.

As is still the case today, the police sought to keep order in the towns and cities. They walked many miles each day on their beats, dealing with traffic jams (there was no Highway Code and keeping to the left had not been introduced), and keeping a lookout for petty criminals, pickpockets and vagrants. By the middle of the century all urban areas had a police force which patrolled throughout the day and night.

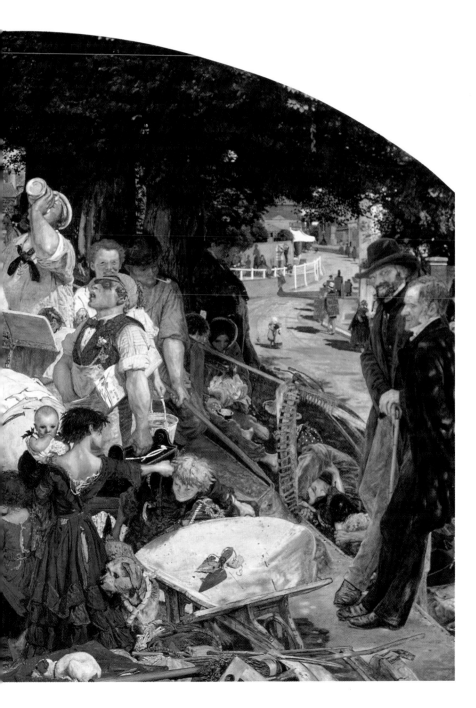

Work *by Ford Madox Brown. How many different activities are there in this painting? What do you think the two men on the right are doing?*

The Coster-Boy

In 1851 Henry Mayhew published a weekly magazine on the London poor as a result of his work as a reporter and investigator. It became one of the Victorian bestsellers:

The life of the coster-boy is a very hard one. In Summer he will have to be up by four o'clock in the morning, and in the Winter he is never in bed after six. When he has returned from market, it is generally his duty to wash the goods and help dress the barrow. About nine he begins his day's work, shouting whilst his father pushes; and as very often the man has lost his voice, this share of the labour is left entirely to him. When a coster has regular customers, the vegetables or fish are all sold by twelve o'clock, and in many coster families the lad is then packed off with fruit to hawk in the streets.

(H. Mayhew, *London Labour and the London Poor*, London 1851)

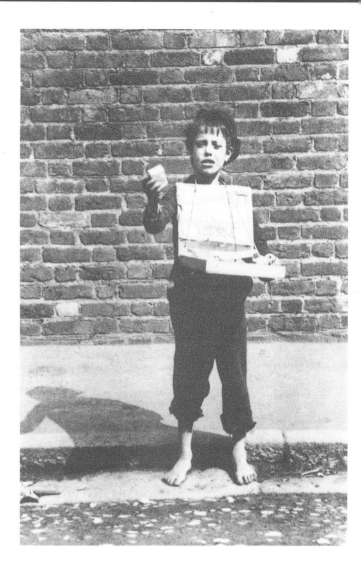

The match boy. Notice his bare feet. The photograph was probably taken to highlight the plight of the young street sellers.

THINGS TO DO

Find out whether your town had a market or a fair. If it still has a market is it still in the same place, and does it specialize in particular goods? Look up your town in a Victorian directory (Kelly's Post Office Directories were published for each county, as were White's) and note down what it says about the markets and fairs.

CAN YOU REMEMBER ?

Why did the poor often shop late on Saturday?
Which Victorian markets still exist today?
Why were there more horses in 1900 than in 1800?
Which city was known as 'the city of 1,000 trades'?
What did Henry Mayhew write about?

CHECK YOUR UNDERSTANDING

Can you remember the meaning of the following words?

cellar dwelling
costermonger
crossing sweeper
drover
shire horse

A Birmingham Jack-of-all-Trades

Birmingham was known as 'the city of a thousand trades'. In these two verses from a popular ballad the man who turns his hand to all types of work is made the subject of a song:

At Islington I sold sky-blue,
In Smithfield was a drover;
In Stafford Street I sold old shoes,
In Bath Street was a glover,
In Loveday Street sold measuring tapes,
In Price Street bled with leeches;
In French Street I sold penny pies,
In York Street sold old breeches.

In Temple Street I sold shaloon (cloth),
In Queen Street a cork-cutter;
In Colmore Street I kept a shop,
Sold, bacon, cheese and butter.
In John Street I sold faggots hot,
Of which I often boasted;
And then in London Prentice Street,
Sold mutton ready roasted.

(Quoted by R. Palmer (ed.) *A Touch on the Times*, Penguin 1974)

List the items or occupations which would have been carried on in the city streets. You will need to use a dictionary to find out the meanings of the unfamiliar words.

The ballad was sold in many of our cities, and the street names would be changed according to where it was sung. Although the extract from Mayhew's magazine provides more accurate detail, why is the ballad a useful source?

A knife grinder was a common sight in Victorian streets.

MAKING ENDS MEET

By 1851 Britain was the leading industrial nation and was able to compete successfully with all its competitors. For the next 20 years those in regular work saw their standard of living improve, as their wages increased ahead of prices. In addition, the Factory Acts brought regulations to industry and improved conditions. For many, the period up to 1870 was a Golden Age.

However between 1873 and 1896 Britain met competition from both Germany and the USA and this contributed towards a depression in both agriculture and industry. Nevertheless, for those in work, wages still kept ahead of prices.

From 1850 working people came to benefit from the lowering of duties on imported goods. For example, the duty on tea fell from 1/10d. per pound in 1858 to 4d. per pound in 1890, and foreign competition and refrigerated ships brought down the price of meat. Factory-produced goods, for example milled corn or canned fruit, helped to keep down prices.

Nevetheless general trends do not indicate how individual families fared. Various reports indicate the problems facing the poor. In 1841, one in twelve people were classed as paupers i.e. those unable to cope without help from the Poor Law or charity. In particular towns, during years when trade was bad, many workers were laid off (sacked) or went on part-time. In 1841, one in three of the adult population of Leeds was without regular employment, whilst in the cotton towns of Lancashire during the American Civil War, the lack of raw cotton meant the closure of many mills. Many workers in towns such as Blackburn had to rely on soup-kitchens, but remained loyal in their support of the Northern States against the slavery of the Southern cotton states.

At a time where there was no state help for the sick or the unemployed, the workhouse was often the last resort. Illness, pregnancy, the death of the bread-winner or old age meant that at certain times virtually all working-class families might fall below the breadline through no fault of their own. Others used their low wages badly and spent their money on drink or gambling which plunged the family into poverty.

Like today, wages varied. In London, wages were higher than elsewhere, and town wages were higher than those in the countryside. Various reports in the first half of the century showed the problems of the poor, but in the 1880s Charles Booth began his survey of the London poor and showed that not only was there poverty in the East End, but there were large pockets of poverty throughout all parts of London as well. Roughly one in three people was classed as poor. These findings were confirmed in a survey of York carried out by Seebohm Rowntree and published in 1901. The results caused a considerable stir because York was considered a pleasant cathedral city.

Thus, for many families, work by the wife and young children was essential to supplement the husband's wage. For many poor families there was the weekly cycle of the money running out before the end of the week, leading to a visit to the pawnbrokers, and the deposit of a wedding-ring or piece of china so that money could be borrowed. When the wage came the article could be bought back on the payment of a high rate of interest.

Not everyone was poor and there were many people – skilled workers, bank clerks, teachers and others who earned perhaps £150 a year – who were able to rent a six-roomed house and who saw their living standards increase. Mrs. Beeton's *Book of Household Management* became the bible of the middle classes and richer groups, whilst more shops, department stores and advertising brought new opportunities for those who could afford them.

Nevertheless, the poor still existed and this fact was brought home to the nation when it was revealed that 25 per cent of the volunteers for the army to fight in the South African War (1899–1902) were unfit for military service. This led the Liberal Government from 1906 to introduce a number of reforms designed to help children, the old and the unemployed.

The Homeless Poor (John Gilbert).
Conditions in the workhouses were so grim that people would only go there as a last resort. Once inside, you were unlikely to get out.

Manchester Workers

Fredrich Engels' father was a German merchant and the son represented him in Manchester in the 1840s. He described those earning just over a £1 a week downwards:

> The better-paid workers, especially those in whose families every member is able to earn something, have good food as long as this state of things lasts; meat daily, and bacon and cheese for supper. Where wages are less, meat is used only two or three times a week, and the proportion of bread and potatoes increases. Descending gradually, we find a small (er) piece of bacon cut up with potatoes; lower still, even this disappears, and there remains only bread, cheese, porridge and potatoes until, on the lowest rung of the ladder, among the Irish, potatoes form the sole food.

(F Engels *Condition of the Working Class in England in 1844* (1845))

A London Widow

When the wage earner died, the family soon plunged into poverty. S.R. Bosanquet writing in 1841 describes how a 40-year-old London widow tried to cope. She had three young children.

> 6 Cottage Place, Kenton Street – Pays 3/- a week rent, owes £1.13/-. Does charing and brush making; earned nothing this week; last week 3/-; the week before 5/8d.

December 15, 1839	*Money spent*	
	s.	d.
Sunday: Bought on Saturday night Potatoes 1½d., bacon 2d., candle ½d., tea and sugar 2d; soap 1½d., coals 2d., loaf 8½d.	1	6
Monday: Tea and sugar 2d.; butter 1½d., candle ½d.		4
Tuesday: Coals		2
Wednesday: Tea and sugar 2d.; candle ½d., wood ½d.; potatoes 1d.		4
Thursday: Coals		1
Friday and Saturday – nothing bought		
	2	5

Received 5 4lb. loaves from the Poor Law Board.

(S. Bosanquet. *The Rights of the Poor* (1841) Quoted by J. Burnett *Plenty and Want* Pelican (1966))

CAN YOU REMEMBER ?

Who were Britain's major trade competitors after 1873?
Why was the trade of Blackburn hit by the American Civil War?
What was the name of Charles Booth's famous investigation?
Which city did Seebohm Rowntree study?
Who wrote 'the bible' of middle-class households?

CHECK YOUR UNDERSTANDING

Can you remember the meaning of the following words?

East End
household management
pauper
pawnbroker
refrigerated ships

Q

What is entirely missing from the goods bought by the London widow? Why do you think that the very poor bought in such small amounts? (Look at tea, sugar and coals.)

THINGS TO DO

It is hard to find out about the average diet, as individuals spend their money in different ways. However, during the nineteenth century more food became available and much of it became cheaper. Try to borrow a copy of Mrs. Beeton's *Book of Household Management* and have a look at some of the suggestions as to how the comfortably-off might spend their money and organize their homes.

Keep a diary of your meals for a week. Organize it as S.R. Bosanquet did in the table in this section. Then list the similarities and the differences between the two. What are the major foods that you eat which were not available in 1901?

The interior of a pawnbroker's shop in the 1890s. The poor would have to pay very high rates to redeem their goods. What reasons would they have had for using these shops?

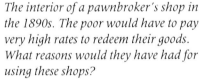

A second-hand clothes shop c. 1900. The majority of the poor would never have new clothes. What can you see for sale?

During the Victorian period the numbers living in large towns of over 100,000 people rose from 1 million or one in ten of the population in 1831, to 9 million or one in four of the population by 1901. By this time three out of every four people were living in urban areas. The main reason for the increasing size of our towns was migration by young people, either single or recently married. Many of these people sought work and tended to group together in areas where rents were low, near to where they might find work.

Throughout the century the demand for accommodation was greater than the supply. The lowest rents ranged from 1/6d. to 5/- a week, with London rents slightly higher. As the better-off moved out to the suburbs, houses which once contained a single family were subdivided, with sometimes single rooms, attics and cellars being rented. With the pressure to build increasing, gardens and market gardens would be built over, and as many houses packed in as possible.

Working-class housing varied according to region. In London there were many courts and alleys in the older areas, whilst as London expanded eastwards rows of terraced houses were built among the factories and by the docks. This area was the least pleasant for building houses as the prevailing wind was from the west and thus many of the noxious (smelly) trades such as bone-crushing and candle-making were located there. Many of the new houses had two rooms up and two down, without internal sanitation, with stand pipes in the streets for water and outside privies serving several houses. Many were built purely for profit before building regulations were introduced, often on poor land without adequate drainage. In extreme cases a dry stream bed would save the builder time in not needing to dig so deeply for cellars or foundations.

In Yorkshire, Lancashire and the Midlands new houses tended to be back to back, where the only ventilation was through the open front door and window(s). This was a much favoured form of building as it enabled the maximum number of back-to-back terraces to be built per acre.

In Nottingham the expansion of the city was made difficult by the surrounding large open fields.

The right to graze cattle on these fields was zealously guarded by local farmers. Thus Nottingham, which had once been described as a beautiful city, found its orchards and town gardens being built on. Three-storey back-to-back housing was built amongst a range of courts and alleys. By the end of the century the city contained some of Britain's worst slums. Conversely, in nearby Leicester land was available for building so the new streets were wide. Working-class housing was rarely more than two storeys in height, whilst the houses usually had four rooms and were occupied by a single family.

Some industrial towns were entirely new. Middlesbrough in the north-east of England began when a group of Quakers bought a 600-acre site and laid out their own town in 1829. By the end of the century a planned iron and steel town had been built to house the work-force.

In Glasgow the wynds (covered alleys) leading into courts were notorious. Housing in the form of tenements, often two or three stories high, was common. With the pressure for more housing, landlords took the opportunity of sub-dividing their properties. One typical example was the conversion of a six-house tenement, each of four apartments, into 21 one-roomed houses. More people could be crammed in and more rent money resulted. In Edinburgh two tenements, which had seven houses and about 35 residents were subdivided, one into 23 houses with 73 residents and the other into 43 houses with 134.

The problems of the poor often increased as town improvements took place. The building of main-line stations, new shopping roads or impressive town halls was usually on land occupied by poor housing. There was no requirement that new housing should be built for those displaced from their homes.

In time towns did gain powers to introduce bye-laws to regulate the standards of new building. From 1875 they were able to purchase and redevelop slum areas. Birmingham was in the forefront of development, but in most towns, slums remained well into the twentieth century, and many were flattened only by Hitler's bombs.

Prince Albert made efforts to improve housing for the poor. Compare this example of his model homes for the poor with the picture below.

Railway arches by London Bridge Station. What dangerous living conditions does the artist portray? (Gustave Doré, 1870)

Slums in Gateshead

Robert Atkinson visited the Pipewellgate and Killgate district of Gateshead where

> each small ill-ventilated apartment of the house contained a family with lodgers in number from seven to nine and seldom more than two beds in the whole.

One house, where he visited a man with children,

> was divided into six apartments, and occupied by different families to the number of 26 persons in all. The room contained three wretched beds with two persons sleeping in each: it measured about 12 feet in length by 7 in breadth; and its greatest height around would not admit of a person's standing erect; it received light from a small window, the sash of which was fixed . . . and the broken panes (filled) with plugs of old linen.

(E. Chadwick *Report on the Sanitary Conditions of the Labouring Population of Great Britain*, 1842)

Overcrowding in London

Thomas Beames quotes a Report giving the effects of the improvements in London and the cutting of New Oxford Street on Church Lane.

POPULATION		
House number	1841	1847
1 (shop)		
2	33	61
3	14	49
4	27	61
5	35	47
6	29	32
7	29	62
8	13	48

(T. Beames *The Rookeries of London*, London 2nd ed., 1852

Add up each column. By how many had these 7 houses increased? Which house saw the greatest increase? What point is Beames making on behalf of the poor when improvements are made?

Glasgow Wynds and Edinburgh Stairs

Dr Arnott visited both Glasgow and Edinburgh in 1840. In Glasgow he described the wynds:

> We entered a dirty low passage like a house door, which led from the street through the first house to a square court (and then) . . . a second and third wynd to further courts.

In these he found that each had its own dung heap. The houses had no privies or drains and the produce of the dung heap would eventually be sold.

In Edinburgh the problem was no better:

> Another defect in this part of Edinburgh is the great size and height of the houses (some of them exceeding ten stories) with common stairs, sometimes as filthy as the streets or wynds to which they open.

Back-to-back housing, like this example from Staithes in Yorkshire, was cramped and unhygienic. Note the bucket, used for collecting water from a stand pipe.

Leeds Back-to-backs

The courts and culs-de-sac exist everywhere. The building of houses back to back occasions this to a great measure. In one cul-de-sac, – there are 34 houses, there dwell 340 persons . . . (during the fairs there are twice that number). The name of this place is Boot and Shoe-Yard, in Kirkgate . . . This property is said to pay the best annual interest of any cottage property in the borough.

(E. Chadwick *Report on the Sanitary Conditions of the Labouring Population of Great Britain*, 1842)

Identify the main dangers to health in each of the extracts on these pages. Why does the Leeds extract explain why it was so difficult to get rid of the slums?

CHECK YOUR UNDERSTANDING

Can you remember the meaning of the following words?

courts
privy
slum
tenement
terraced houses

THINGS TO DO

1 The worst Victorian slums will now have been demolished, but if you look at a nineteenth century Ordnance Survey map of your area you will see where they were. Look out for narrow roads or streets and names such as alley, court, lane. The shape of the back-to-backs and the courts will be recognizable on a 25-inch scale map.

2 The local library will have the 1841–91 censuses on microfilm and you will be able to see how many people lived in a particular yard or street, say in 1851. Compare it with the 1861 census. Have the numbers increased? Are the same people still living there? What jobs did they do?

CAN YOU REMEMBER ?

How many people were living in towns by 1901?
Why was the East End of London less popular than the West End?
Why were back-to-back houses considered unhealthy?
Which city could not expand into its surrounding fields?
Which city was founded by the Quakers?

In the Victorian period, houses were usually rented, rather than bought, and people moved house as frequently as today.

In the village or small town, rich and poor lived close to each other, but in the rapidly growing towns and cities, those who could afford to often moved out into the suburbs. Here the new homes were cheaper and not so densely packed together.

Thus the West End of London and Edgbaston in Birmingham were laid out for the wealthy on land where once there had been fields, small-holdings or market gardens. Sometimes a landowner would deliberately break up his estate for development. In the Victorian suburb of Bickley, some 12 miles from London, the local landowner, William Dent, who was also the Chairman of the Mid-Kent Railway Company, laid out part of his estate near the new station for housing development. When the project was complete, as well as large villas being built with coach-house and stabling, a cricket field and a church had been erected. The first owners were wealthy city businessmen, owners of factories, architects and barristers all attracted to a pleasant area, conveniently close to London by train. The census returns show a range of domestic servants, sometimes as many as 12, in one of the larger houses.

Local advertisements in the surburban press stressed the speedy and frequent rail services to London, the open spaces, and sometimes the prestige of the areas. Links with royalty or lords were always good selling points.

Semi-detached villas were popular amongst the middle classes. In Bromley, Kent, five- to seven-bedroomed houses were built in Hope Park in 1880 which were advertised for rent from £80 – £105 per year.

However, not only the upper and middle class moved out of the city. Camberwell in South London saw much building of houses for clerks and skilled workers renting comfortable one-family houses. Many walked across the bridges to work in London each day, or caught the horse-drawn omnibus.

When you go out to investigate the houses in your town remember that a large Victorian house was built for one family and its servants. Today many are too large for modern families, and many are sub-divided into flats or used as offices. In addition, the garden may have been reduced and part of it used for further building. In the 1960s and 1970s many Victorian houses were demolished.

Many of those that remain are now in conservation areas and cannot be taken down. However, over time many houses have been re-roofed with different materials; and woodwork, windows and doors replaced, sometimes in quite a different style from the original.

A detached house built in Bromley, Kent, in the 1880s.

THE HOMES OF THE RICH

Suitable Town Houses

Throughout the period, many books were
published on housing, furnishings and the
necessary servants according to your income.
Here are some excerpts from a book by J.H.
Walsh in 1857:

The 16-roomed house   Cost: £1200 – £1800

By carrying storey over storey a large and roomy house
may be constructed, composed of 16 rooms, besides
dressing rooms, and quite sufficient for an ordinary
family. In it are good-sized dining and drawing rooms,
with eight bedrooms, in addition to two servants' rooms
in the roof . . . The kitchens are underground . . .

The 10-roomed house   Cost: £800 – £1000. Let at £55
per year

Intended to afford a much more limited accommodation . . . much is sacrificed to economy; but still, for a
small family, it may be made very comfortable.

The 4 and 6-roomed house   For those of annual income
of £100 – £200 per year

They are composed simply of a basement – ground and
first floor, in each of which there are two rooms.

(J. H. Walsh *A Manual of Domestic Economy Suited to
Families spending from £100 – £1000 a year*, 1857.
Quoted in Rubenstein, D. *Victorian Homes* David &
Charles, 1974)

Walsh was describing house prices in London.
The suburbs would have been cheaper. Small
suburban houses would have been lived in by
people such as skilled mechanics, various
experienced clerks and teachers. Rent would be
between 10/- and 12/6d. per week. For the others
rent would be about a tenth of the price of the
houses.

CAN YOU REMEMBER ?

Which groups moved into the wealthy suburbs?

Why did Camberwell develop as a London suburb?

Why do we know so much about who lived in each house between 1841 and 1891?

Why was the railway so important to the development of the suburb?

Where would the servants' quarters be situated in the house?

Advice for furnishings

There were many books of advice on how to furnish a home. These are a selection from the 1860s:

Carpets: Next to the effect upon a visitor of the entrance hall, the carpets of the rooms to which he is introduced gives the first impression of the house to him. They are the fundamental feature of the furnishing – the background of the picture.

Artificial lighting. Gas, cheap, brilliant, convenient, but finding a rival in the mineral oils produced from the earth itself; and a succeeding generation will doubtless see . . . in the 20th century, and of a more perfect science than our own – the grand force of electricity.

(*Artistic Furnishings and Home Economy* Ward Lock (c 1865))

THINGS TO DO

Try to find a directory for your area. Try to identify some of the houses; the house names may still remain, but be wary about the numbers which may have changed. In the roads where infilling (houses built in gardens) has taken place, or the houses demolished to make way for flats you may have difficulty. Nevertheless, if you take a Victorian road where the houses are still mainly standing, with the help of a directory and large-scale Ordnance Survey maps you should be able to do some interesting detective work. You could use the 1851 and 1881 censuses and the local library might have some old photographs. Also talk to older people who may remember the area as it was before more recent changes.

A suburban Victorian villa. Note the size of the gardens and compare it to the picture of poor housing on page 25.

Do you agree with the author about the importance of carpets? Can you spot the reference to the oil lamp?

CHECK YOUR UNDERSTANDING

Can you remember the meaning of the following words?

domestic economy
mortgage
semi-detached

PUBLIC HEALTH

In the late 1830s the Government was increasingly aware of the problems of the poor in the rapidly expanding slums, and the increasing number of deaths caused concern. A detailed enquiry was commissioned which reported to Parliament in 1842. The Report on the *Sanitary Condition of the Labouring Population of Great Britain* was written by Edwin Chadwick. It made clear the problems and dangers to health. It quoted extensively from reports sent in by the Poor Law doctors from throughout the country. After reading it no one could be unaware of the dangers and the likelihood of an early death in our towns and cities. The table below made this clear.

Even within a particular town, death rates varied enormously. Those at most risk lived in the densely-packed low rent slums, which were to be found in virtually all towns and cities. Chadwick's report, and subsequent ones, are full of instances of overcrowded, badly built, poorly maintained buildings. Where cellars were rented out and when houses were 'run up' cheaply on marshy ground or below the water level, there was damp, and the cellars might often be flooded not only with water, but also with sewage from leaking cess-pits. Slum houses were rarely connected with the water mains of the private water companies. The stand pipes in the streets only supplied water for so many houses a few hours each day. Very few houses in the slums had any internal toilet facilities and privies were usually in a shed and shared by many families. The waste was removed by 'night soil men' who sold what they collected to local farmers for fertilizer.

Added to this, the narrow streets and alleys in the slums had no drains and were rarely paved, so much of the refuse, human, vegetable and animal, was heaped in them. The smell must have been unbearable.

Closely-packed alleys and courts prevented sunlight from entering, and back-to-back housing with no through draughts, prevented adequate ventilation.

In towns and cities which had grown up alongside rivers such as London, Nottingham, Salford and Leeds, the rivers were not only used for dumping refuse, but also by the local water companies for water.

Until the 1880s it was believed that many diseases were spread by smell (the miasmic theory). Later it was found that cholera and typhus were waterborne.

In industrial towns the smoke pollution from the coal fires was added to by the smoke from the many factory chimneys, causing a constant haze over low-lying towns. Buildings were blackened and individuals were harmed by lung and chest diseases. Inside the factory or workplace risks to limbs were common because of unguarded machinery. In the cotton and woollen mills lungs were damaged by the fluff which was constantly in the air. In Sheffield the grinders spent their day grinding cutlery and agricultural equipment such as scythes, over dry stone grinding hulls in small workshops. They were very well paid but many died young from the dust they absorbed into their lungs.

LIFE EXPECTANCY IN 1842 Different groups					Average age of death		
	Manchester	Bolton	Bethnal Green	Leeds	Liverpool	The rural county of Rutland
Professional persons, gentry and their families	38	34	45	44	35	52
Tradesmen and their families	20	23	26	27	29	41
Mechanics, labourers and their families	17	18	16	19	15	38

What conclusions would you draw from this table? Look both across and down the columns.

Despite these hazards, it was generally felt that Governments should not interfere and decide how employers should act. The first Factory Act of 1833 was a start, and the first of many, but there were insufficient inspectors to see that legislation was carried through.

Chadwick's report was not acted upon, partly because of cost and also because the Government did not want to impose upon employers. Instead, they delayed by commissioning a further report. *The Health of Towns Report* of 1845 surveyed 50 of our major towns and confirmed many of Chadwick's findings.

Between 1831–32, 32,000 people died of cholera, but it was not until the outbreak of 1848–49, when 62,000 died, that any notice was taken. Not only were people shocked by the numbers, but also by the fact that roughly half of those attacked, died usually within days. What was worrying was that the disease hit the slums worst, but then spread to all classes.

Applicants for Admission to the Casual Ward *by L. Fildes. There was little real provision made for the poor in Victorian times.*

In 1848 a Public Health Act was introduced which allowed parishes to form a Local Board of Health if the death rate was particularly high. Once elected, it could levy a rate which would pay for improvements and introduce bye-laws. In time Medical Officers of Health were appointed to advise the Board of Health and many towns set up drainage and sewerage schemes for their area, and began to lay down standards for new building. This enabled the large cities and towns to deal with their various problems centrally, but there were always those who did not wish to have high rates. Nevertheless, in time many of the problems which Chadwick had exposed were remedied, but by 1901 much more remained to be done.

Lack of Water

A report of 1850 by Dr Hector Gavin outlined the problems faced by the poor in Jacob's Island, Bermondsey, London, a slum on low-lying marshland, close to the Thames:

> (women) may be seen at any time of the day, dipping water with pails, attached by ropes to the backs of houses, from a foul foetid [stinking] ditch, its bank coated with a compound of mud and filth, and strewed with offal [unused parts of animal] and carrion [dead flesh of an animal], the water to be used for every purpose, culinary [cooking] ones not excepted.

This was made worse by rubbish being thrown into the same ditch from the houses.

> I was also informed, that during summer, crowds of boys are to be seen bathing in the putrid [rotten] ditches . . .

Water supply was a real problem. In the same Report Mr Bowie investigated Cooper's Court, Blue Anchor Yard. He found 246 people

> supplied from a ½-inch tap, for an hour, or say two hours, not including Sunday, the water running a part of the time so slowly as to take a quarter of an hour to fill a two-gallon pail.

(*Report on the Supply of Water to the Metropolis* Appendix III)

Does the second extract help explain why the women in Jacob's Island drew water from the ditch?

A COURT FOR KING CHOLERA.

CHECK YOUR UNDERSTANDING

Can you remember the meaning of the following words?

cholera
night-soil
offal
tradesman

How many hazards to health can you identify to justify the artist's title?

THINGS TO DO

1 List five of the places inspected by the MOH and explain why each might be a health risk.

2 After reading this section and those earlier in the book you will see that health might be endangered by any one or more of the following:

air pollution
poor building
lack of ventilation
dampness
lack of toilet facilities and sewers
lack of powers available to the town to take action
overcrowding
poor drainage
poor drinking water
lack of good water supplies
dangerous conditions at work
lack of knowledge on dangers to health

Check back in the book and find examples of three which you think were the most important.

CAN YOU REMEMBER ?

What was the average age of death for a labourer in Bethnal Green in 1842?
Why were cellar dwellings so unhealthy?
Why did death rates vary so widely in towns?
Why was the miasmic theory wrong?
What were the duties of the Medical Officer of Health?

Air Pollution

A report of 1843 described Manchester:

nearly 500 chimneys, discharging masses of the densest smoke; the nuisance has risen to an intolerable pitch, and it is annually increasing, the air is rendered visibly impure, and no doubt unhealthy, abounding in soot, soiling the clothing and furniture of the inhabitants, and destroying the beauty and fertility of the garden as well as the foliage and verdure [green] of the country.

(*Select Committee on Smoke Prevention* 1843)

Q

What health problems would be faced because of pollution? Compare this account with the illustration of Birmingham on page 6. Does one support the other?

Improvements in Inspection

Much progress in public health had taken place by 1901:

The range of duties of the MOH [Medical Officer of Health] included inspecting common lodging houses ... cellar dwellings, garret dwellings, stable dwellings, canal boat dwellings, tents, caravans and sheds, and insanitary houses or areas, places where food is produced and prepared or sold, as slaughter-houses, cattle and other markets, retail premises, cow-houses, dairies and milk shops, bakehouses, and school premises, various kinds of workshops, premises where the various offensive trades are carried on, nuisances, smoke, overcrowding, dampness, and many others too numerous to mention.

(Dr John Sykes, 1894. Quoted by A. Wohl *Endangered Lives*, Dent, 1983)

A Medical Officer of Health was a doctor appointed to advise on the public health problems in a particular area.

EDUCATION

Education was neither compulsory nor free until the last decade of the nineteenth century. The growing population of London, with its increasing number of young families and children, led to the establishment in 1817 of a Select Committee on Education in the Metropolis. The main concern was the need to keep law and order and to prepare children of the lower orders for work.

Education for the children of working people was largely in the hands of two voluntary religious societies. The largest was the National Society which was Anglican and provided Church of England schools. The other was also Christian but did not follow any sectarian (particular) view. It was called the British and Foreign School Society, and was supported by chapel-goers. Both societies used the Monitorial System which was based upon a one-teacher school. The teachers were trained according to the principles of Andrew Bell and Joseph Lancaster, and were trained in issuing commands and learning the system by which they drilled older children as monitors, who in turn drilled groups of younger children. Based upon rewards (prizes and badges) and punishments the

schools could cater for 300–400 children who would be taught the basics of arithmetic, reading and writing. Much of the reading and writing was from the Bible. Within a few years hundreds of Monitorial schools had been established in Britain's cities and towns. They were financed by voluntary contributions and by small contributions of a few pence per week from the parents. The education given was very limited but was better than nothing. It was certainly better than the Dame schools, run by older women in their own homes, which were little more than child minding.

Dame schools like this one were generally a haphazard and inadequate means of education.

For the middle and upper classes, there were a range of schools, all fee-paying, although some which had been founded in the sixteenth or seventeenth century with money left for their foundation, enabled children from quite poor homes to attend. These were known as grammar schools. At the top of the scale were public boarding schools for the children of the rich and the new professional classes.

In 1858 the Newcastle Commission was appointed to enquire into the state of popular education in England. The report is in three large volumes and provides a wealth of information on the education which the majority of children in our towns and cities received. The main recommendation was for a Revised Code by which schools were to be given grants according to the number of children and their performance in annual examinations, to be conducted by a Government Inspector.

In 1870 an Education Act was introduced which enabled school boards to be formed in areas where there were insufficient school places. Once a school board was formed it could levy an education rate, which would be used for building Board schools and for paying teachers. Many of the two- and three-decker older schools in Britain's towns and cities date from this period, and can be recognized by the stone plaque giving the Board school name and the date of its foundation. The first and the largest of these was the London School Board formed in 1871.

In time Boards began to appoint Attendance Officers to ensure that the children went to school. The Board schools filled the gaps in the existing voluntary system. By 1900 with compulsory education up to a minimum school leaving age of 12, all children were receiving a basic elementary education. However, secondary education for all did not come until the twentieth century. The majority of children did not have the opportunity to gain sufficient education to go into the professions or to university.

Ages at School

In a report of 1844 an inspector listed the entrance and leaving ages of selected schools that he had visited. They were all Church schools (i.e. national schools):

Manufacturing and Mining Places

Name of school and place	Age of entrance	Age of leaving
Leeds (St. George)	3	12
Leeds (Christ Church)	5	12½
Gateshead	7	11
Leigh National School	6	11
Bolton (Trinity)	6	10½
Salford (St. Matthews)	7	12
Holybridge (St. Paul)	6½	12½
Heywood (St. Luke)	3	12
Hull (St. Stephen)	6	11
Newcastle (St. John)	7	12½
Carlisle (Trinity)	7	12

Note that these are selected schools. The inspector also discussed problems of frequent truancy. He included a conversation with the Vicar of a Salford Church:

> **One third of his population changed their homes *annually*. The operative factory worker population, allured from their homes in prosperous times by high wages, or driven in times of distress to change their abodes in search of employment... the children of course move too, and the school career commenced in one place, and broken through removal, is perhaps never again renewed.**

Other children left school only to work in industries not covered by the Factory Acts:

> **early interruption to school-progress arises from winding bobbins – an occupation of children from 8 and 9 years of age which prevails in Manchester and other neighbouring places.**

Even the 1844 Factory Act was unsatisfactory. Under this Act children under 13 working in textile factories had to attend school part of the week. They were called part- or short-timers:

> **Where others are clean in person and neat in dress, and happy in expression – these are dirty and labour-soiled, in ragged and scanty clothes, with heavy eyes and worn faces. In the clothing districts, their faces, necks and hands, are deeply stained with the blue of the dye used for the cloth. From the spinning mills they come covered with the 'fluff' from the yarn – their hair thickly powdered with it – tangled, especially that of the girls, as if no comb could ever penetrate it.**

Many estimated that on average children received no more than 100 weeks schooling at this time. What would be the major problem facing a short-timer in school, both from the child's point of view and the teacher's?

A cookery class taking place in a Board School in 1885.

CAN YOU REMEMBER ?

What were the names of the two largest school societies?
What did the Newcastle Commission recommend?
What was a School Board?
Who were 'short-timers' and why were they so called?
What sort of information was contained in a school log book?

CHECK YOUR UNDERSTANDING

Can you remember the meaning of the following words?

sectarian
metropolis
monitorial system
Revised Code
voluntary system

THINGS TO DO

1 Many National and British schools still survive and are used as Primary Schools. From 1870 onwards Board schools were built and many of these two- or three-decker schools survive in our towns and cities. The local directories will contain a list. See how many of them still survive.

2 Log-books are a fine source of information. Old schools may still have them, or they may be in the local library. If so, see what was happening in your school. Look up the years 1887, 1897 and 1901. All these dates relate to the Queen. Also check the winter months and the month of July to see if there are any references similar to those at Raglan.

Raglan Board School, Bromley

Head teachers were required to keep a school log-book (a daily diary). Raglan was a school in the Bromley School Board formed in 1888:

2nd April, 1890 I completed my examination of the school this afternoon. The result is very satisfactory. Great progress has been made in all subjects. Spelling and arithmetic are still weak and the proportion of bad readers in Standard I (the lowest) though lessening, is still great.

However, truancy and poverty were still problems:

13th June, 1890 I find that several boys are sent out on Fridays by their parents to sell weekly papers ... The attendance is still low despite our efforts. The most common excuse is that the child has been kept at home to mind the baby while parents go to work.
29th June, 1890 Fruit-picking has commenced and has had a bad effect on the attendance. Find that some go without parents' permission.
13th January, 1891 Severe weather and poverty of parents affect the attendance. Many away on account of having no boots to come in such weather.

(*Raglan Schools' Centenary 1889–1989* Published by the school, 1989)

The Newcastle Commission

The Report in 1861 generally criticized the methods of education. Too much was learned by rote (memory) without understanding, and standards varied too much. The outcome was the Revised Code. Nevertheless, there was evidence submitted to the Committee of the great benefits of education. A letter from Burton-on-Trent commented favourably on their National school:

Thirty of the boys have obtained good situations; either in the railway or in the breweries ... Eighty have gone out as apprentices to good trades ... and are on their way to become valuable members of society.

The education given has borne fruits in the district – less swearing, less immoral conversation, less indecent scrawling on the walls, and an improved more religious tone.

For many working people the beer house or public house was the centre of their social life. Unlike their overcrowded homes, these places provided warmth, light and company and drink was a means by which many were able to escape from the daily cycle of long hours at work. Drink was also a recognized problem and as the century proceeded Temperance groups emerged which encouraged people to sign the Pledge and abstain from alcoholic drink. It was not only the effects of drink upon health, but the waste of precious money which caused concern.

The Victorians banned many sports which they regarded as barbaric. Thus cock-fighting and bear-baiting were ended. Dog-fighting and cock-fighting continued illegally in the backs of public houses in the poorer areas, and much gambling took place. Boxing was also popular, and from the 1860s football came to be played on a national basis with the creation of leagues. Similarly, cricket, athletics, bowls and rowing became popular. Many of the teams grew up as works teams, for example, West Ham United, formed in 1895, was the Thames Ironworks team, hence their nickname 'The Irons' or 'The Hammers'.

The growth of leisure activities and holidays is closely related to various factors. When working

The choice of entertainment was incredibly varied for those who could afford it. What is happening in the far left of the picture?

hours were long, life was one long cycle of work and sleep. In time, hours of work came to be regulated and reduced, and half-days on Saturday afternoons became common. In 1871, Bank Holidays were introduced, so that for one day at Easter, Whitsun and in August factories would be closed. In the industrial North whole towns came to close down for a week in the summer, enabling the factory workers to take their holidays. These 'wakes' weeks would see virtually the whole town going off by special trains to seaside resorts, such as Blackpool. Holidays were as yet unpaid and workers contributed towards Holiday Clubs to save for their annual treat.

The other essential element, apart from increased time, was money. In the second half of the century real income began to rise (pay rises kept ahead of the cost of goods) which gave the well-organized surplus money to spend. Finally, there was cheap transport in the form of the railways. The Railway Act of 1844 required companies to provide three classes of travel, with the third costing 1d. a mile. Soon the railway companies were offering Cheap Day Returns to the races or the seaside.

Blackpool rose from a sandy coastline on which a few fishermen lived into the leading seaside town of the north-west, drawing thousands each year from the grim terraced streets of the Lancashire cotton towns. With the popularity of bathing and sea air, its sea and beaches provided open spaces and pleasure; piers, theatres and aquariums were provided to attract the visitor and seaside towns began to compete with each other. Towns began to cater for different groups: Blackpool had far more lodging houses than Brighton, and into these were crammed working-class families. Brighton, on the other hand, had far more hotels. Eastbourne, Bournemouth and Bognor were aimed at a higher-class visitor than Yarmouth, Skegness, Southend and Blackpool, which catered for the town workers.

The railway guaranteed the success of the Great Exhibition in 1851, and cheap days were organized for working people who travelled on cheap returns from all parts of Britain. Similarly, the growth of the Football League and county cricket was aided by improved transport.

The Egyptian Hall was renowned for its entertainments in the late nineteenth century.

Many towns and cities also had theatres. The middle class criticized the Penny Gaffs in the East End of London, where for a penny brief plays and sketches were given, often in rooms or public houses. In addition, from the 1860s music-halls became popular, as were light operas, made popular by Gilbert and Sullivan. Penny Readings and recitals were also a favourite form of entertainment.

Public libraries and swimming baths were provided by local councils, and in some cases were aided by charities, such as the Carnegie libraries. Forward-looking towns provided open spaces within their boundaries: Leicester, Preston, Manchester and Sheffield were all examples of towns which had parks which were free for all. In these parks, boating lakes, bowls and open air bandstands were all provided for the people.

LEISURE AND SPORT

Derby Day

A Frenchman described Derby Day on Epsom Downs. He travelled from Waterloo by train:

> Epsom course is a large green plain, slightly undulating, on one side are reared three public stands and several other smaller ones. In fact, tents, hundreds of shops, temporary stables under canvas, and an incredible confusion of carriages, of horses, of horsemen, of private omnibuses, there are perhaps 200,000 human heads here.
>
> ... It is a carnival, in fact; they have come to amuse themselves in a noisy fashion. Everywhere are gipsies, comic singers and dancers, shooting galleries where bows and arrows and guns are used, ... games of skittles and sticks ... and the most astonishing row of cabs, barouches, droskies, four-in-hands [all carriages] with pies, cold meats, melons, fruits, wines, especially champagne. They unpack; they endeavour to sell you penny dolls, remembrances of the Derby ... to black your boots. Nearly all of them resemble wretched, hungry, beaten, mangy dogs, waiting for a bone, without finding it. They arrived on foot during the night ... the majority of them have bare feet and are terribly dirty ...

(H. Taine *Notes on England* 3rd ed. 1872)

Music Halls

Charles Booth describes the popular music hall:

> Music halls appeal to a far larger class of pleasure seekers than theatres. Prices are not so high, and the entertainment provided does not as a rule, demand an undivided attention. You can smoke and drink at your ease while the entertainment is going on, for a ledge fixed at the back of the seat of the man in front serves as a table on which to place your glass.
>
> ... The great difference between an actor in a theatre and a music hall 'artiste' is that whereas the first has his part provided for him, the second has to depend upon his own individual efforts and abilities.

(C. Booth *Life and Labour of the People in London*, 1889)

Actors in music halls often did an 'act' in three different music halls in one evening. There were usually up to 90 acts in one performance.

Why would a music hall actor have to have very different talents from those in the theatre?

In spite of what Taine said why did both the rich and the poor enjoy their day?

THINGS TO DO

Buildings often change their use over time. Many bingo halls today were once cinemas or even theatres. Every town had its theatre and music hall. Find out if any of the buildings still survive.

Try to find out whether your favourite sport or leisure activity was practised in Victorian times. You will be surprised how many people watched sport in the later part of the century, especially athletics, cricket and football.

CHECK YOUR UNDERSTANDING

Can you remember the meaning of the following words?

lodging houses
the Pledge
temperance
wakes week

CAN YOU REMEMBER ?

Why is the West Ham United team known as 'the Hammers'?
When was the Bank Holiday Act introduced?
Why was the Railway Act of 1844 so important?
Why were seaside holidays so popular with town workers?
When was the Football League formed?

The Football League

In 1888 the Football League was founded. The original twelve members were:

Accrington, Aston Villa, Blackburn Rovers, Bolton Wanderers, Burnley, Derby County, Everton, Notts County, Preston North End, Stoke, West Bromwich Albion, and Wolverhampton Wanderers.

Professional football had been made legal in 1885. With the help of an atlas, find out where the original teams came from. What do all these towns have in common?

A rugby match from 1879. How does it compare with a contemporary match?

What can you remember?

Where did King Cotton rule?

Which was the largest ship canal joining two northern cities?

What do Swindon, Crewe and Ashford have in common?

Where was the Great Exhibition held?

In what occupation were the majority of women and children employed?

What is a sweat shop?

What did Smithfield Market specialize in?

What did a pawnbroker do?

Who wrote *The Book of Household Management* and why was it so popular?

Why was living in slums dangerous to health?

Why was Edwin Chadwick so important?

In what year did 62,000 people die of cholera?

Where did northern industrial cotton workers spend their holidays?

What made the Football League possible?

TIME CHART

1837	Accession of Queen Victoria
	Population of London 1.75m (1831) – only 6 other towns over 100,000
1842	Edwin Chadwick's *Report on Sanitary Conditions of the Labouring Population* brings Public Health to a wider public
1842	Mines Act – Children and women could no longer work underground
1845	*Health of Towns Report* – covers 40 largest towns
1844, 1847, 1850	Factory Acts – each reducing hours of work
1847	Liverpool, the first town to appoint a Medical Officer of Health
1848	Public Health Act – Boards of Health could be established
1848–9	Cholera – 62,000 died
1850	Preston forms a local Board of Health
1851	Population of London, 2.25 m, Liverpool next largest with 375,155
	Great Exhibition in Hyde Park, London
	Henry Mayhew publishes *London Life and London Poor*
	Singer produces first advanced sewing-machine
1857	Hugh Miller makes tour of England
	Sheffield, the oldest football club formed
1858	Act of Parliament gives town councils power to make bye-laws
1861	Newcastle Commission on Education reports
1862	Revised Code for schools. Payment by Results
1861–5	American Civil War – causes cotton famine in Lancashire
1865	London's main drainage scheme completed
1867	Factory Acts extended to cover small factories and workshops
1870	Education Act – School Boards could be formed
1871	Football Association Cup (F.A. Cup)
1875	Artisan Dwelling Act – councils enabled to raise rates to clear slums
1876	Minimum age of employment – 10-years-old
1888	Football League introduced
	Beatrice Webb works in a sweat shop
1889	First volume of Charles Booth's *Life and Labour* published
1894	Blackpool Tower opened
1899–1902	South African War (Second Boer War)
1900	*Daily News* holds 'Sweated Goods' Exhibition
1901	Rowntree publishes York study
	Population of London 4.5 m
	Queen Victoria dies. Edward VII King

44

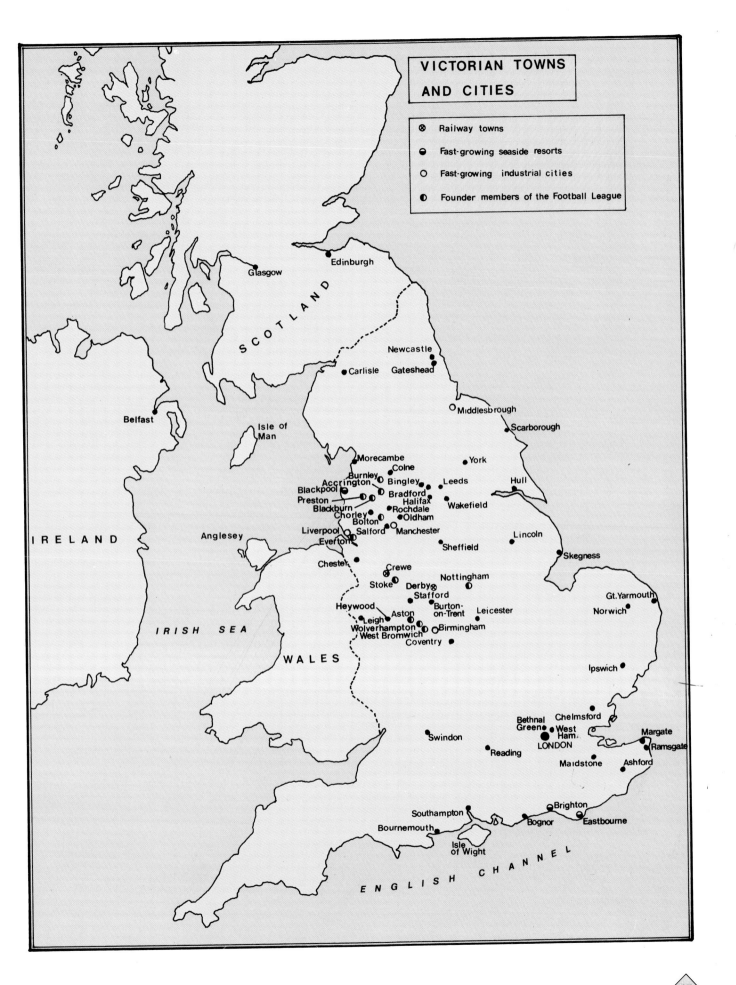

VICTORIAN TOWNS AND CITIES

⊗ Railway towns

⊖ Fast-growing seaside resorts

○ Fast-growing industrial cities

◐ Founder members of the Football League

SCOTLAND

Glasgow

Edinburgh

IRELAND

Belfast

Isle of Man

Carlisle

Newcastle

Gateshead

Middlesbrough

Scarborough

York

Morecambe

Colne

Burnley

Accrington

Bingley

Leeds

Hull

Blackpool

Bradford

Preston

Halifax

Wakefield

Blackburn

Rochdale

Chorley

Bolton

Oldham

Liverpool

Salford

Manchester

Everton

Lincoln

Anglesey

Sheffield

Chester

Skegness

IRISH SEA

Crewe

Nottingham

Stoke

Derby

Gt. Yarmouth

Stafford

Norwich

Heywood

Burton-on-Trent

Leicester

Leigh

Aston

Wolverhampton

Birmingham

West Bromwich

Coventry

Ipswich

WALES

Chelmsford

Bethnal Green

West Ham

Swindon

LONDON

Margate

Reading

Ramsgate

Maidstone

Ashford

Southampton

Brighton

Bournemouth

Bognor

Eastbourne

Isle of Wight

ENGLISH CHANNEL

Anthrax   A dangerous disease which affects both animals and humans

Bengers food   Baby food

Board schools   Schools paid for out of the rates and run by an elected School Board

Carnegie, Andrew   Scottish emigrant to the USA who became very rich and gave money to various charities, including the building of public libraries in Britain

Census   Information collected on a particular day every ten years since 1801 (except 1941). Personal details are not available to the public until 100 years after their collection, but general details are published soon afterwards

Cities and Towns   Cities are larger than towns, and in the nineteenth century a town may have expanded into a city. A city usually had its own Lord Mayor and a cathedral

Directories   These contain excellent local information. By the 1860s every county had one giving details of all towns and villages. They may be inaccurate or out of date, but they give an excellent broad picture of the time

Drove roads   Also known as green roads. These were the tracks along which animals and livestock would be driven to market. Many still survive today and they are often walled on either side. In the North they often went over hills, and were apart from the ordinary roads over which carriages and coaches travelled

Garret dwellings   Rooms in roofs or attics which were rented

Gazeteers   See **Directories**

Green roads   See **Drove roads**

Hand-looms   These were operated by workers at home. In factories, rows of power-looms were installed which were powered by water. Later, steam power was used. In the factory the workers tended the machinery and did not need to be as skilled as the workers at home. At first cotton spinning was done in the factory, and weaving was done at home. The hand-loom weavers suffered when weaving machinery was used in the large factories

Migrant   Someone who moves from place to place, usually within his or her own country. Most migration took place over short distances, and much of it was into the towns and cities

Offensive trades   Ones which gave offence, in smoke, smell and other forms of pollution

Poor Law   In 1834 a new Poor Law Act was passed. It was designed to try to force those able into work. If an 'able-bodied' man wished for relief (financial help) he could receive it only in the harsh workhouse. When the system was extended to the north of England in 1836–7 industry was in the midst of a depression and many workers were laid off through no fault of their own. Workhouses were introduced, but outdoor relief still had to be given

Privies   Toilets, usually a hole in the ground

Retail premises   Shops

Revised Code   Means of testing standard of education. Six standards were laid down in the basic subjects. Children were tested on them at the annual inspection. Children could leave school when they had reached the third standard

Rookery   The Victorian word for a slum, where the poor would be packed together

Soup kitchen   Where the poor could go for food; often soup and bread. The rich people often gave the poor tickets for the soup kitchen rather than money. The soup kitchens were often run by religious groups and relied on charity

Stand pipe   Water pipe in the street or court, especially in the poorer districts

Tenement   A building which would be divided into various sections, called apartments in Scotland. Today they would be called flats

Villa   The word is used in a variety of ways. A pair of pleasant homes with three bedrooms each might be called villas. Equally, a large detached house with a large garden would also be called a villa. What they both have in common is a garden

Whitworth, Joseph   (1803–87) Worked as a mechanic at various Manchester machine manufacturers. Later began own tool-making business. From 1840–50 he produced a measuring machine so that screws and gauges could be precision made. Soon he was able to reproduce screws, lathes and various other accurate machine tools. He also invented the muzzle-loading rifle

Wynd   A covered way, under an existing building leading into a court

FURTHER READING

There are few books which are written on Victorian towns in general. However, you will find two series particularly useful. The *Then and There* series by Longman has a number of titles which will enable you to follow up several topics in more detail. For example, the one by R. Watson, *Edwin Chadwick and Public Health* (1969) draws on materials from both Darlington and London, whilst P. Searby's *The Chartists* centres on Leicester.

The second series which will provide many examples of sources is Batsford's *Finding Out About* series. Titles which refer to towns include *Victorian Towns, Victorian London, Victorian Health and Housing, Industrial Britain, The Poor in Nineteenth-century Britain, Victorian Law & Order* and *Victorian schools*.

The first starting point should be your local history library. You may well find a history on your actual town, or the library may have produced a series of documents or photographs. It is useful to find out general information about the area before you start asking specific questions.

The following are some of the books which helped me in writing this book:

Beeton, I., *Book of Household Management* Ward Lock, 1892
Burnett, J., *Plenty and Want*, Pelican, 1966
Burnett, J. (ed.), *Useful Toil*, 1974
Chadwick, E., *Report on the Sanitary Conditions of the Labouring Population of Great Britain*, 1842
Engels, F., *Condition of the Working Class in England, 1844*, 1845
Howarth, E.G., *West Ham*, Dent, 1907
Mayhew, H., *London Labour and the London Poor*, London, 1851
Palmer, R. (ed.), *A Touch of the Times*, Penguin, 1974
Rowntree, B.S., *Poverty: A Study of Town Life*, 1901
Rubenstein, D., *Victorian Homes* David & Charles, 1974
Taine, H., *Notes on England*, 3rd ed., 1872
Wohl, A., *Endangered Lives*, Dent, 1983

Acknowledgements

The Author and Publishers would like to thank the following for their kind permission to reproduce illustrations: The Mary Evans Picture Library for pages 1, 6, 7, 9, 10, 11, 14, 20, 21, 25, 27, 30 and 38; The Museum of London for pages 4 and 5; the Bridgeman Art Library for pages 12 and 33; e.t. archive for pages 36, 37, 40, 41 and 43; and Robert F. Brien (illustrator) for the map on page 45.

The cover illustration shows *Work* by Ford Madox Brown, and is reproduced by kind permission of Manchester City Council.

Thanks go to the *How It Was* series editors for advice and editorial input: Madeline Jones, Jessica Saraga and Michael Rawcliffe.

INDEX

Page numbers in **bold type** refer to illustrations.